Let's Go to a World's Fair

Here is the story of how fairs developed from early times to the present. You learn what fascinating new inventions were first shown at world's fairs, from the London Crystal Palace to the 1964 New York fair. You see how every fair has its own way of showing what is new and exciting in the world.

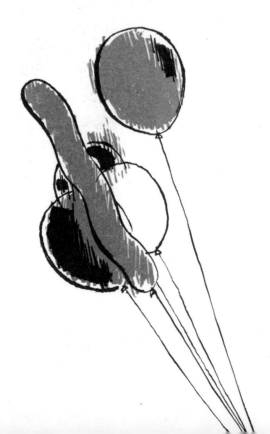

Let's Go to a

World's Fair

by ROBERTA S. FEUERLICHT

illustrated by ROBERT BARTRAM

G. P. PUTNAM'S SONS   NEW YORK

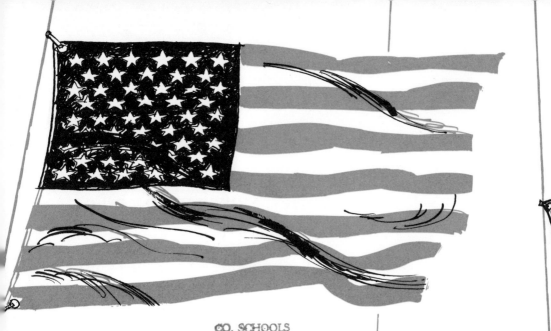

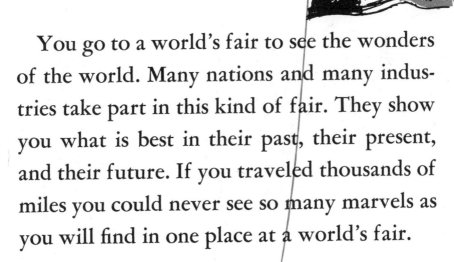

You go to a world's fair to see the wonders of the world. Many nations and many industries take part in this kind of fair. They show you what is best in their past, their present, and their future. If you traveled thousands of miles you could never see so many marvels as you will find in one place at a world's fair.

World's fairs are not new. The first one was held more than 100 years ago. But long before there were world's fairs, there were smaller gatherings called fairs. People have been going to fairs for thousands of years.

The first fairs were places where men from different tribes met to trade food and clothing. They were like markets, but there was

one important difference. A market is a place where people from the same neighborhood come to buy and sell goods. But fairs are for strangers. People often travel great distances to go to a fair. Fairs are usually larger than markets and they are held only at special times.

In ancient times, fairs were usually held at holy places. First, people came to these places to worship. Then merchants came to sell the worshipers food and cloth and trinkets. Sometimes jugglers or acrobats did their tricks for the crowds. In this way, religious festivals often turned into fairs.

This kind of religious fair lasted for many hundreds of years. Sometimes merchants sold their goods right in the churchyards.

About 1,000 years ago, during the time called the Middle Ages, fairs began to change and to get larger. People went to fairs mostly to buy and sell goods.

In Europe, the first great fairs during this time were held at Champagne, in France. Nearly all the merchants in Europe traded at the Champagne fairs. Some traveled for months to bring their goods there.

There were six fairs at Champagne, one after the other. Since each fair lasted two months, there was some kind of fair at Champagne all year long.

You could buy nearly anything at the Champagne fairs. There were booths with linen and leather, spices and shoes, wheat and wool. And you could have fun, too, listening to singers called minstrels or watching acrobats and puppet shows.

PUPPET SHOW

For hundreds of years, there were many great fairs all over Europe. Then, in the 1700's, the steam engine was invented. It was the beginning of the age of machines. With these new machines, everything began to change, including fairs.

Soon it was no longer necessary for merchants to go to fairs to order goods. They could order them by telegraph. It was no longer necessary to see everything you bought before you bought it. Since goods were made by machines, every piece was made the same way.

For a while, fairs were no longer very important. People went to them mostly to have fun. Many kinds of circus and carnival acts

PIG THAT TELLS FORTUNE

were first seen at fairs. There were acrobats, trained bears, giants, dwarfs, magicians, and tattooed ladies. One fair even had a pig that could tell your fortune.

Then, in 1798, some men in Paris decided to have a new kind of fair. It would show the different kinds of goods made by machines. People would come not only to buy but to learn. They would learn about the new machines and the new products being made.

The fair was a success. Many people came to see it. After that, Paris had a number of fairs like this. So did other countries. But each time, just one country took part in it.

One year the Royal Society of Arts in London decided to have a fair like the ones in Paris. Then a man named Henry Cole had an idea. He wanted to invite France to take part in the English fair. He felt it would be interesting to show English and French goods side by side so everyone could see both kinds.

THE CRYSTAL PALACE

Then Cole thought about his idea some more. He decided it would be even more exciting if many countries took part. And that is how the first world's fair was born.

Cole told his idea to the President of the Royal Society of Arts. The President was Prince Albert, the husband of Queen Victoria of England. Prince Albert agreed that Cole had a wonderful idea. From that time on, the Prince worked as hard as he could to make the first world's fair a great success.

A man named Joseph Paxton designed the building for the fair. He made it out of glass and iron, and someone named it the Crystal Palace.

Many people laughed at the Crystal Palace. They said it would leak and the visitors who came to the fair would get wet. They said the glass would be broken by the first hailstorm. They said the whole building would be blown over by the wind.

But none of these things happened. Prince Albert and Queen Victoria liked the Crystal Palace. And some people thought it was the most beautiful building in the world.

The first world's fair opened on May 1, 1851. If you had been there that day you would have seen Queen Victoria and Prince Albert. With them were their two oldest children, Victoria, who was ten, and Edward, who was nine.

The Queen wore a pink and silver dress, with many diamonds. When she arrived at the Crystal Palace, cannon roared and trumpets

QUEEN VICTORIA

blared. The crowds sang the British national
anthem, "God Save the Queen." Everybody
cheered.

The Queen and Prince Albert led a procession from one end of the building to the other. It was so exciting that some people cried. Then the Queen had a nobleman named Lord Breadalbane announce that the fair was open. After Queen Victoria left, the crowds poured in.

You could have seen more than 15,000 exhibits at the first world's fair. They came from many parts of the world. A famous rare diamond, the Koh-i-Noor, came from India. It was shown in a large gold birdcage, built on a thick stand. Every night the diamond was hidden inside the stand because the police discovered that some thieves planned to steal it.

Walking around the Crystal Palace you could have seen many models of ships, lighthouses, and bridges. Railroads were still a new invention then, so there were several locomotive engines and a lot of railroad equipment. But perhaps your favorite exhibit would have been the silent alarm clock. It woke you up by turning your bed on its side.

Half of the Crystal Palace had exhibits from England, and half had exhibits from other nations. Canada sent sleds and birch-bark canoes. France showed fine silks and carpets, and beautiful gold and silver pieces.

America was still a young country, and did not have very much to exhibit. But you could have seen Cyrus McCormick's new invention, the reaper. It was a machine for cutting and harvesting grain. The American exhibit also had false teeth, chewing tobacco, and Colt's revolver.

And if walking by all these exhibits made you hungry, you could stop at a stand and have ices, or some lemonade.

CYRUS McCORMICK'S REAPER

The Crystal Palace exhibition was open for 140 days. During that time, over six million people came to see it. Many people came over and over again.

Queen Victoria visited the Crystal Palace about 50 times. She often took her children with her. She thought the fair was one of the wonders of the world and said that she wished she could see it every day.

The first world's fair was a great success. People discovered that a world's fair was a place where every country could show its very best. It was a place where everyone could see what everyone else was doing. A world's fair was a place to learn and to have fun.

FALSE TEETH

COLT'S REVOLVER

Since 1851, there have been hundreds of world's fairs. They have been held in many different countries. Some have been large and some have been small. Many of the large ones were held in America.

America's first world's fair was large but it was not as good as the English world's fair. In 1853, a group of Americans tried to copy the Crystal Palace exhibition. They built a new Crystal Palace in New York City. It stood on Sixth Avenue and 42nd Street, behind the place where the Public Library now stands.

The New York Crystal Palace was not very successful. It was not built as well as the first Crystal Palace. When it rained the roof really did leak and everybody did get wet.

The next world's fair in America was much better. It was held in Philadelphia in 1876, in honor of the Declaration of Independence.

The exhibits at the Philadelphia fair were shown in many buildings instead of one. These buildings are called pavilions. There were 167 pavilions at the fair in Philadelphia. In one of them you could have seen a man named Alexander Graham Bell. He was showing his new invention, the telephone.

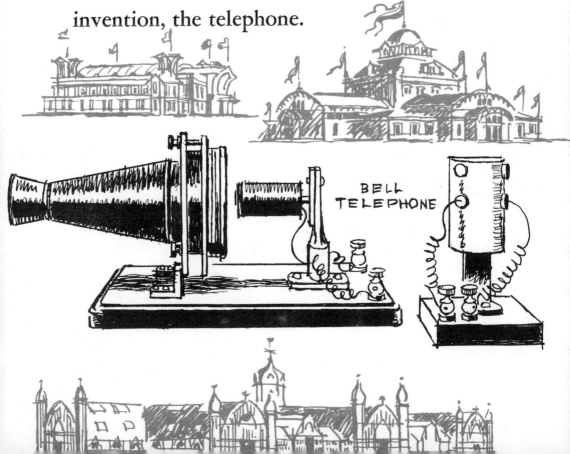

BELL TELEPHONE

In 1893, there was an even greater world's fair in America. It was held in Chicago, and nearly 30 million people visited it. There were many interesting new inventions there, but the most important was the electric light bulb.

You might have been even more excited by another new invention, the Ferris wheel. It had 36 coaches, and each one held 60 people. But so many people wanted to ride on the Ferris wheel you always had to wait in line for it.

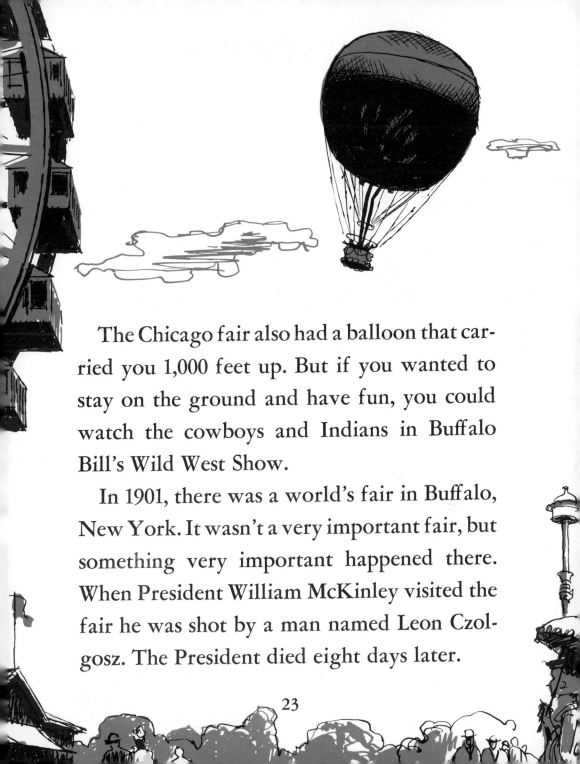

The Chicago fair also had a balloon that carried you 1,000 feet up. But if you wanted to stay on the ground and have fun, you could watch the cowboys and Indians in Buffalo Bill's Wild West Show.

In 1901, there was a world's fair in Buffalo, New York. It wasn't a very important fair, but something very important happened there. When President William McKinley visited the fair he was shot by a man named Leon Czolgosz. The President died eight days later.

In 1904 there was a large world's fair in St. Louis, Missouri. The newest invention then was the automobile. There were 100 autos on exhibit in St. Louis.

Some very popular foods were first served at the St. Louis fair. You could have a snack of hot dogs and iced tea, or a grilled hamburger on a bun.

Because the first world's fair in Chicago was so good, Chicago had another fair 40 years later, in 1933. It was the first world's fair where science exhibits were very important. You could see a transparent man with the parts of his body lit up. And you could gaze at a balloon for exploring the skies and a bathysphere for exploring the seas.

In 1939, there were two world's fairs in America. One was in New York City and the other was in San Francisco.

The San Francisco fair was on an island built right into San Francisco Bay. It was called Treasure Island, and you could get to it by ferryboat.

The San Francisco fair told all about the western states of America and the lands of the Pacific Ocean. One of the most interesting exhibits was an old Japanese castle. But if you wanted to watch something really American, you could see the rodeos.

The fair in New York City was in Flushing Meadow Park, where the world's fair is today. Many of the exhibits at the New York fair told about the world of tomorrow. The new invention that everyone found most exciting was television.

The fair had a symbol which became very well known. It was a long, thin building called the Trylon and a small, round one called the Perisphere. You could go into the Perisphere and see a city of the future. It was called Democracity.

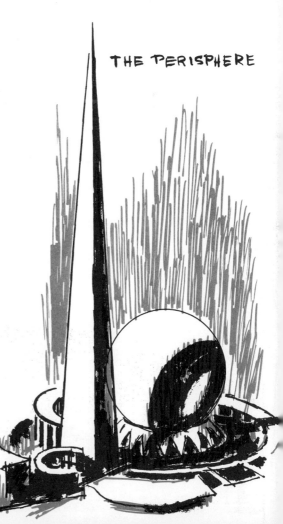

THE PERISPHERE

But the exhibit you might have liked best was the Children's World. There you could see animals and toys, a circus and a cave of jewels. You could take a trip around the Children's World on a small railroad train and learn how people live in many different nations.

The next important world's fair was in Europe. It was held in Brussels, Belgium, in 1958. By this time the world had changed a great deal. The newest discoveries were atomic energy and flights into space. In the Russian pavilion at the Brussels fair you could see the first spaceship that ever went around the earth.

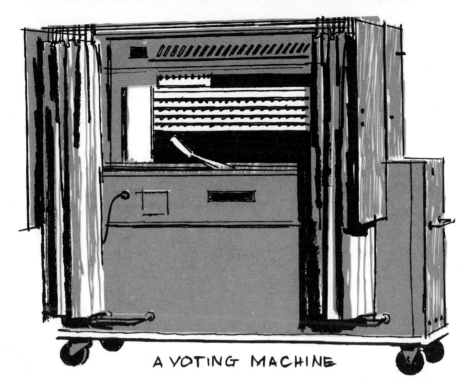

A VOTING MACHINE

The American pavilion showed a clock run by atomic power. It also showed what life is like in America. There were voting machines, newspapers, and comic strips. There was even a drugstore where you could buy an ice-cream soda.

Perhaps you were able to go to the world's fair that was held in Seattle, Washington, in 1962. If you did, you saw the tall tower called the Space Needle. The Space Needle was the symbol of the Seattle fair. There was a restaurant at the top that turned very slowly. As you ate you could see the fair from all directions.

THE SPACE NEEDLE

Many countries and industries had exhibits at the Seattle fair. The most popular exhibit was the Science pavilion built by the United States government.

One of the exhibits in this pavilion was a Junior Laboratory of Science. It was for young people only. At first adults were allowed to come in. But so many of them came, the children could not see the exhibits. After that, only children and teachers could visit this part of the pavilion.

One of the things you could learn in the Junior Lab was how much a grapefruit weighs on the sun, the moon, and the different planets. You could also see how a telescope works and how to measure distances in space.

About 10 million people visited the Seattle world's fair. Some 70 million people will see the New York world's fair which runs from April to October in both 1964 and 1965.

This fair is in Flushing Meadow Park, where the 1939 New York fair was held. Its symbol is the Unisphere. The Unisphere is a model of the world made out of stainless steel. It is 140 feet high. There are three steel rings around the Unisphere which are held in place by wires that are nearly invisible. Lights flash along the three rings, to give the feeling of satellites in orbit around the earth.

There are many pavilions at the fair, with thousands of exhibits. Most of the pavilions were built by one country or one company. In a few pavilions you will find exhibits from several countries or companies.

It takes a lot of time and money to build a pavilion at a world's fair. Some of them cost many millions of dollars.

THE UNISPHERE

First, a pavilion is planned by someone called an architect. He makes a drawing of it called a design. Architects design all kinds of buildings, but fair pavilions are not like the buildings people usually live and work in. That is because fair pavilions are put up for a short time only. After the fair is over, most of them are torn down.

For this reason the architect can design very modern and unusual pavilions. He can experiment with new shapes and materials. As you look around you at the fair, you can see how different the pavilions are from your school or home.

After an architect designs a pavilion, it is built by a construction company. Then a man called an exhibit designer decides what will go inside. After he designs the exhibits, they are built by special companies that do nothing but build exhibits for fairs and shows of all kinds.

The many thousands of exhibits at the New York world's fair cover everything from the life of the past to the life of the future. In Dinoland you can see life as it was millions of years ago. There are nine full-size models of dinosaurs in Dinoland. Three of the models have moving parts.

One of the dinosaurs is the Brontosaurus, the largest land animal that ever lived. He was

BRONTOSAURUS

about 70 feet long. The Dinoland exhibit is right near a highway called Grand Central Parkway, and if you ride through the fairgrounds on the Parkway, you can look up and see the giant Brontosaurus.

Many of the exhibits at the fair show life in the future. In the Travel and Transportation pavilion you can pretend to explore the moon. A moving ramp takes you around the rim of a moon crater. While you are on the moon you will see a team of lunar explorers at work drilling the soil and building places to live.

The exhibits at this world's fair are divided into five main areas. One is all about transportation. You will find Dinoland and the moon exhibit in the area on transportation.

Another part of the fair is for industry. Many businesses, both large and small, have exhibits there. If you want to get hungry, you can go to the World of Food pavilion. There you can see a supermarket of the future, a New England fishing village, and a model of Hershey, Pennsylvania, where chocolate candy is made.

If you visit the Bell Telephone pavilion you can ride a comfortable chair through an exhibit that tells you all about communications. It is the history of the many ways in which men have talked to each other, from the drums of the cave man to signals in space.

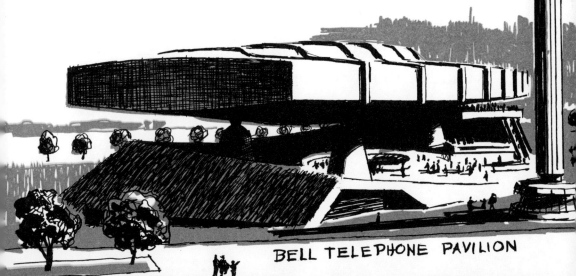

BELL TELEPHONE PAVILION

When you see the latest telephones in the Bell pavilion try to remember that Alexander Graham Bell showed his first telephone at the world's fair in Philadelphia less than 100 years ago.

A third part of the fair is called the international area. It is for exhibits from different countries of the world. One of the largest pavilions was built by Indonesia. Part of the exhibit is the tower of a temple. The tower was brought to America all the way from Indonesia.

A wide avenue leads from the main entrance of the fair to the Unisphere. This is called the Avenue of the Americas. On both sides are pavilions built by Latin-American countries. One of the most beautiful is the Mexican pavilion. It looks as if it is floating in space.

Switzerland is another of the many countries with exhibits at the fair. You may want to take a Swiss sky ride. It takes you over the fairgrounds in small cars, 100 feet above the ground. You can see the whole fair at once from one of these cars.

U.S. GOVERNMENT PAVILION

The fourth area of the fair is for the exhibits built by the United States government and by the states. The government has a huge building with glass walls. It is 20 feet above the ground.

Most of the states have exhibits which tell about their people and history. In the Maryland pavilion there is a theater where you can see the battle of Fort McHenry. It was during this battle that Francis Scott Key wrote "The Star-Spangled Banner."

New York State has its own pavilion and so has New York City. The New York State pavilion has three tall observation towers from which you can look down at the fair. In the New York City pavilion you can watch ice-skating shows.

NEW YORK STATE PAVILION

The Missouri pavilion has a famous plane,
the *Spirit of St. Louis*. In this plane Charles
Lindbergh was the first man to fly alone across

the Atlantic Ocean. Missouri is also showing
some of the ships in which men will fly
through space.

The fifth part of the fair is the lake area.
This is mostly for fun. There you will find a
circus, a wax museum, and several theaters.

There are exciting shows of water, lights,
and music in the lake area. It is also the place
to go if you want to take a boat ride. You have

your choice of boats. You can ride in an out-rigger canoe, like the Hawaiians, or in a gon-dola, like the people of Venice. There are also boats with glass bottoms.

The lake area also has a boat you cannot ride in. It is a model of one of the most im-portant boats in American history. This is the *Santa María,* the ship on which Columbus

GONDOLA   SANTA MARIA

sailed to discover America. The model is full-size. It has flags, weapons, and a crew made out of wax.

Even though the fair is divided into five main areas, you can find many special exhibits all over the fairgrounds. There are five pavilions built by religious groups. In the Vatican pavilion you can see one of the most beautiful

THE PIETA

statues in the world. It is called the "Pieta," and it was carved more than 450 years ago by a great artist named Michelangelo.

The next important world's fair will be in Canada in 1967. It will be on an island in the St. Lawrence River, near the city of Montreal.

Men are already at work planning this fair. It takes years to put together a world's fair you want to see again and again. And if they are successful, it will be such a wonderful fair that you will never forget it.

WORLDS FAIR 1967

GLOSSARY

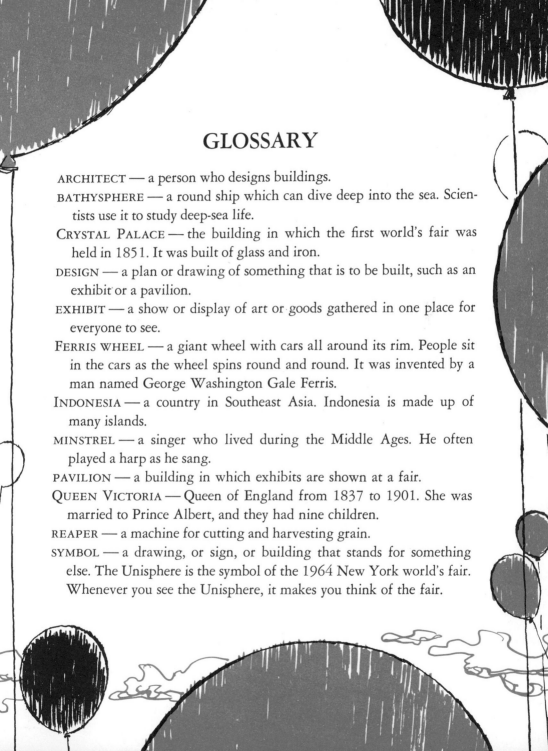

ARCHITECT — a person who designs buildings.

BATHYSPHERE — a round ship which can dive deep into the sea. Scientists use it to study deep-sea life.

CRYSTAL PALACE — the building in which the first world's fair was held in 1851. It was built of glass and iron.

DESIGN — a plan or drawing of something that is to be built, such as an exhibit or a pavilion.

EXHIBIT — a show or display of art or goods gathered in one place for everyone to see.

FERRIS WHEEL — a giant wheel with cars all around its rim. People sit in the cars as the wheel spins round and round. It was invented by a man named George Washington Gale Ferris.

INDONESIA — a country in Southeast Asia. Indonesia is made up of many islands.

MINSTREL — a singer who lived during the Middle Ages. He often played a harp as he sang.

PAVILION — a building in which exhibits are shown at a fair.

QUEEN VICTORIA — Queen of England from 1837 to 1901. She was married to Prince Albert, and they had nine children.

REAPER — a machine for cutting and harvesting grain.

SYMBOL — a drawing, or sign, or building that stands for something else. The Unisphere is the symbol of the 1964 New York world's fair. Whenever you see the Unisphere, it makes you think of the fair.

OTHER TITLES IN THE POPULAR *LET'S GO* SERIES

Science
   for a Nature Walk
   to a Planetarium
   to a Rocket Base
   on a Space Trip
   to a Weather Station
Health
   to a Dentist
   to a Hospital
Communications
   to a Telephone Company
   to a Television Station
Food and Clothing
   to a Bakery
   to a Candy Factory
   to a Clothing Factory
   to a Dairy
   to a Farm
Commerce and Industry
   to an Automobile Factory
   Logging
   to an Oil Refinery
   to a Rubber Plant
   to a Steel Mill
Transportation
   to an Airport
   to a Freight Yard
   to a Harbor
Conservation
   to a Dam
   to a National Park
American History
   to Colonial Williamsburg
   to Mount Vernon
Armed Services
   to Annapolis

   to the U.S. Air Force Academy
   to West Point
Government — Local
   to a City Hall
   to a Court
   to Vote
**Government — National and
      International**
   to the Capitol
   to the F.B.I.
   to the Supreme Court
   to the United Nations Headquarters
   to the U.S. Mint
   to the White House
Recreation
   to an Aquarium
   to a Circus
   to a World's Fair
   to a Zoo
Music and Art
   to an Art Museum
   to a Ballet
   to a Concert
Community — Commercial
   to a Bank
   to a Garage
   to a Newspaper
   to a Supermarket
   to Watch a Building Go Up
Community — Government
   to a Firehouse
   to a Library
   to a Police Station
   to a Post Office
   to a Sanitation Department
   to a School